LEAP

LEAP

JORDAN HARTT

TEBOT BACH • HUNTINGTON BEACH • CALIFORNIA • 2015

Leap

The editors, Tebot Bach, and the authors wish to thank the journals and publications where some of these poems previously appeared, sometimes in slightly different forms. And, of course, very special thanks to David St. John.

Book design: Michael Wada
Cover Art: clker.com
Author Photo: Anne WIlliams

ISBN 10: 1-939678-17-X
ISBN 13: 978-1-939678-1-71

Library of Congress Control Number: 2015944581

A Tebot Bach book
Tebot Bach, Welsh for little teapot, is a Nonprofit Public Benefit Corporation, which sponsors workshops, forums, lectures, and publications. Tebot Bach books are distributed by Small Press Distribution, Armadillo and Ingram.

The Tebot Bach Mission: Advancing literacy, strengthening community, and transforming life experiences with the power of poetry through readings, workshops, and publications.

This book is made possible through a grant from The San Diego Foundation Steven R. and Lera B. Smith Fund at the recommendation of Lera Smith.

www.tebotbach.org

Some of the pieces in this book first appeared, often in different forms, in the following journals: "Leap" in *Press 1*; "The Owl" in *The Gallery*; "Three Men" and "Beaver Valley Homestead—1966" in *Two Hawks Quarterly;* "Loon" in *The Crab Creek Review;* and "Quiet Water" and "A Final Memory" in *Prose Poem.*

Contents

For the Elwha

i once seen a man turned into a bear

                                            was a family used to live here name a
reisenauer

                th father, name a dean, was th best damn logger ever lived, in my
book

          no one knew where he come from, had a kinda southern accent, but he
wasn't th kinda guy you could ask questions a

                             just showed up on th side a th road
one morning holdin a chainsaw n swung inta th cab a one a them
rayonier trucks free n easy, grinning face white as sunbleached driftwood

   had long skinny arms like cables n used to sharpen the teeth a his chainsaw
inta th shape a diamonds ever night, n all the other men tried it but it didn't
work for em like it did for him

                        he won th county logging tournament ever year,
 pullin and pushin a saw or runnin his husqvarna, perspiring heavily, though i
wouldn't call it sweat

                    married a local gal, myrtle arnold, n their son miles
followed him inta th woods at th age a seventeen

                           miles was th spittin image a
his father, right down to th way they walked, slightly stooped over, always
hitchin up their pants, as if in a hurry to get somewhere

                             but they talked slow,
lethargic, suspenders taut against rail–thin shoulders

                        when miles was th age a
   twenty, a cedar twisted th wrong way on him, n broke his head like a glass jar
    that evening dean knelt in his caulked boots in front a th unlit fireplace,
hands shaking so much that matches fell scattered all around him on the thin
hard carpet

                n th next day he knelt in front a th old cedar cross at the small
wooden chapel a christ sanctified up on th hill n started carrying a hymnal
with him to th hills ever morning, n wouldn't let his youngest son, howie, leave
school for the forest

                   (i remember howie sittin in the wet backyard turnin his
older brother's baseball glove over and over in his hands, n putting his face into
it, n smellin it)

            knowin myrtle couldn't have beared to lose howie too

                              but dean
changed after miles die in another way too, n nothin howie did was as good
as miles, in his father's eyes

                  howie had big shoulders like massive boulders, like
logs, n growin into a body like that, had no coordination, was always knockin
things over

I.

The rotting stumps
Of an abandoned dock are glued to the sky.
Ships cling to the fringe like bits of lace.
There is no earth.

—*Colleen J. McElroy, "Winters Without Snow"*

Leap

the woman who jumped or fell from the bridge onto the rocky sandbar of the
 river jumped or fell during the middle of the   cold day   cold white sky
feathered plumes of smoke rising through the forest from hidden
cabins   mossy roofs thick as sponges   river shining like a handful of
quarters   dull sun white as a peeled potato

the woman who jumped or fell from the bridge onto the rocky sandbar of the
river still carried within herself the stillbirth of her daughter and the earthen
cry of shovel blade as she buried the paleness of her daughter's body, more
salmon than human, beneath the muddy soil, firs bending in the wind
overhead

the woman who jumped or fell from the bridge onto the rocky sandbar of the
river climbed up over the restraining metal fence and leaned out holding the
cable and then slipped or let go, still carrying within herself the memory of
howie and the way she'd thrown beer in his scarred face, weeks earlier, still
thinking about the way he'd punched her in the stomach, months earlier, still
thinking about his sweater that smelled of salmon and tobacco, the way he'd
duck under the firs in the backyard, bend his head into his hands and click his
lighter until the puff of smoke exhaled into the cold air, releasing him, the rain
falling on the plastic toys of her sister's children and the swingset and the
mossy plastic pool with standing rainwater pregnant, she jumps on the
trampoline

the woman who jumped or fell from the bridge onto the rocky sandbar of the
river felt the cold cable in her hands thick as an alder slicker than she'd realized
her weight pulling her hard toward the river, hard toward the earth   she
jumped or let go saw white sky   mist moving through firs   alders
   cottonwoods   plumes of river rushing past the rocks and in that brief
instant remembered fishing with howie   remembered the taut fishing line
   in that brief moment she remembered the rocking of the aluminum boat and
the way howie had stood up as if to steady it   she remembered the strength of
the salmon's tug against the nylon line   she remembered the sky and the forest
and the river shining like quarters

so let's remember the salmon, too   the salmon hooked on the end of her
nylon line   let's remember the flashing lure that catches her eye   the
flashing lure that glints in the roof of the ocean like herring   the miracle of

salty flashing herring near the lid of the water where water gives way to
emptiness and absent sun

yes, let's remember the salmon who emerged out of the egg   the roots of
cottonwoods grasping the slippery mud   the sun splintered in the shallow
water   the wide mouth of glaciers long-since melted   murky rocks and
stripes of watery sunlight   gills   let's remember her pilgrimage to the sea
the headlong pour from the river into the ocean   the continental shelf
disappearing beneath her   the bodies of the salmon slowly separating like
spilled matchsticks in the great openness of the ocean

yes, let's remember the salmon and the fierce tribal march toward the aleutians
    let's remember salmon woman's periodic leaps from the ocean into
the sky like the joy of a pregnant woman in a mobile-home park jumping on a
trampoline   let's remember that upward jump   the quick paddle to the
surface and the leap and whistle of air over gills   let's remember the curving
hanging sky

let's remember the salmon woman and the human woman and the maturation
of the salmon woman   the sudden heat in her veins as she looks at a male
    who knew those fierce tribal mouths could cause such storms in her cartilage
    lust   swelling of abdomen   the sudden urge to turn homeward for spray and
spawn   their very bodies changing the mouths of the males curving deeper
    the silver, the blue of their bodies growing deeper   let's not forget the
hunger of the migration   the loss of food her body growing thinner let's
remember hunger and lust and water and the turn homeward

and let's remember the lure   the bland rubber taste of the lure   the sudden
hook in the roof of her mouth   the jerk upward toward the empty sky
    she twists, turns, thrashes and longs for the ocean   she
remembers the great pink migration and openness of the water and the
coppery lust for men and the lust of men and she thinks of the slick roots of the
cottonwoods and remembers the taste of freshwater and she fights and she's
lifted into the pure air a squall of gray on the horizon   saltwater rains from
her body down to the swells of ocean as she fights   there's a sudden loosening
    a tear in the roof of her mouth   the taste of her own blood and bone
and metal and she falls free

yes, let's remember the salmon   remember her upstream fight into the
freshwater   let's remember what it means to climb up pure rushing river
    a fight for inches   the world a tear of bubbles of air and water   let's
remember what nine hundred miles of struggle means to a salmon   let's

11

remember rushing water and dams and hooks and the paws of bear   she
fights for the final scrape of her fin on home gravel   for the sharp taste of
blood in the water   for the ecstasy of reddish eggs the spray of watery milt
over eggs   the muddy bare roots of the cottonwoods   the fading red sun the
dimming of the earth the dimming of the water   the reach of the claws of bear

but of the golden beer running down howie's bearded face let us (or let us not)
forget the way that he looks at her without talking and the way he wipes his
face the rain slumping against the roof of the tavern   the pulse of the
jukebox rattling the wooden floor   the bartenders polishing the smooth cedar
flank of the bar with dirty rags   their black hair draining all the way to the
floor   all the way to the sea   let us or let us not forget the way that
howie wipes his face with a flannel sleeve and the fierce way he looks at her
and she stands yes she rises yes and she puts her purse over one shoulder and
she walks out yes and he sits there and wipes his face with a flannel sleeve and
then he feels something animal rise inside him

let's remember that some men only pretend to be men but are grizzly bears in
the shape of men   he runs after her, in his haste slipping down the rain-s
oaked steps   he roars in the rain   the tail-lights of her truck kick away
from him like a salmon kicking upstream   he screams like a bear   he roars
like the sound of a car crash   drunk he roars and no one in the bar bothers
him because they know that bears roar because that's what bears do (and as
for the woman, well, they're just glad she got away)

the woman who jumped or fell from the bridge onto the rocky sandbar of the
river had jumped on the trampoline earlier that day under the black swaying
telephone wires   the phone was ringing in the mobile home   fallen alder
leaves were rotting by the fence   the whole earth was rusting in the rain   she
leaped and the sky was white and she opened her mouth to the rain   she
swallowed the metallic taste of the rain and she leaped and she held her
outstretched arms to the sky and she held her arms to the rain and the mist and
the rotting alder leaves and the long wet grass that grew up through the
cracked plastic toys and the spokes in the rusted tricycle and she leaped in the
air and came down hard on the wet grass and she lay crumpled in a pile of
knees and elbows and laughter but let's not remember her fall   and let's not
remember her fall from the bridge either   let's remember her leap   ecstatic
    a salmon, in the white smoky air

The Owl

owl trapped between the bald moon and forgetful blankets of snow
        dark blood runs between owl's fingers motor oil strains
between owl's callused fingers   cold wrench   the snow falls around owl's
truck   he's on his back on the ground changing the oil   sky white and
close by   snow falling   the radio shorts out cold   owl remembers
changing the oil

owl remembers dancing coldness giving way to the warmth of the tavern
the bodies in flannel pitched in hard against one another blood the
color of rust on his fingers   pitchers of beer   heads of animals on the cedar
walls   owl lifts off the snowy branch a flurry of snow falls to the
ground   owl remembers anne's tongue-colored dress

he remembers the rust-colored snow   owl remembers their silent hunts
together   he circles against the cold bald moon blue-black sky   silent bodies
of firs   owl remembers motor oil   remembers blood
   remembers anne packing the truck with her bags   remembers the way they
stood, cold sifting down around them   owl remembers the flakes of snow
settling on her tongue-

colored dress hat and sweater   she gets in the truck   drives uphill
away from him   a mouse darting across the white snow   life is lived
forward understood backward, owl thinks   the element of flight triggers him
and he dives   heart pounding wings silent
   earth silent under the blankets of snow   she drives uphill, away from him

the taste of copper in his mouth he lurches after her her truck lodged stuck in
the snow   tires spinning   he runs into the cabin he grabs a carbine rifle

      bullets   his hands shake   bullets spill onto the hard cedar floor like
icicles breaking   he skids outside   he sees the tires of her truck flinging snow
into the air as she presses the accelerator   in panic he lugs his body up the hill,
heart pounding inside him

blood flowing through him owl lifts off in flight   what does it take to forget,
he wonders   how much time   how much whiskey   the injections
of how much ephedrine and pseudoephedrine into his veins   how many
mice   how many bald moons
   how many freshly fallen blankets of snow   how many skeletal firs   how
many metamorphoses how many silent flights does it take to forget

*the mouse turns left, right   owl nestles the mouse in his talons   owl feels the
terrified tongue-colored heart in his talons   owl lifts through empty
branches   the heart beating wildly   the brain protects the heart by
forgetting what it has to forget to survive   owl rises weightless, silent, above
the treeline toward the cold bald moon*

Three Men

hood of blank sky a white man dragged
behind a ford wrists tied to a strong rope

in the truck cab two men drink rainier
beer the wailings of jimi hendrix drown

out the screams of the dying man
they bury him above a riverbank two

deer watch silently chewing leaves with
blank glassy eyes skeletal white bodies

of streamside cottonwoods standing in
careless witness as the final shovel-

fuls of wet earth are tossed on the pale
limp body

he misses his wife for a brief instant
thinks about the way she would plant

tulip bulbs in the damp earth in front
of their mobile home yard

full of fishing net and styrofoam buoys
piles of cedar firewood sleeping underneath

mossy blue tarps he remembers the
softness of her hands she'd been

broken somehow years earlier and now
everything about

her was soft and gentle—she even drove
slow, he remembers kidding her, just

there is a moment, at
the end, where he

thinks of god, the
way he thinks of

the sky: distant,
and sometimes it

rains, and sometimes
it does not, and some-

times two men drag
a third behind a rusted

ford toward the river
where they bury him

deep in the muddy soil

he (this is the third man)
notices that the sky has

opened up today; that
the clouds have, thank god,

thinned, letting pale
sunlight leak through; that

dark green trees flash by
he thinks of his son's gaunt

face and loud motorcycle,
and the way he would

watch television, at night,
as if willing the noise to

above a whisper

drown out the sometimes
overwhelming pain

II.

trees river rope sky
dust truck wheels fir

as they drink beer, not talking about that
day where they'd met the man in the diner and

trees flashing by in
silent accomplice

the way he'd looked at them and then, finding out
what his last name was, visiting on him the sins of

streamside cotton-
woods, sullen wise

his grandfathers, not talking about that day
where the light had been gray and soft leaking

ford screeching on
tires on the road

down from what some men refer to as heaven and
others the sky, not talking about the screech of the

above the flashing

tires as he, the driver, ground

river glimpsed
through thin trees

to a halt above the elwha and untied lifeless
hands from a rope he never remembered what

bears the awful
weight of the sun

happened to that rope had he put it in the truck
bed or thrown it in the river or tossed it into the

tell me the story
of two men who

overwhelming ache of the hole
with the dead man he didn't remember, nor did

dragged a third man
behind their truck to

he ever talk about it, not even with the other man
or the streams of wives and girlfriends who

the elwha and buried
that third in the dull

passed through his life
instead he drank and barbecued and played

wet earth above the
rock-studded water

softball, and it were as if the thing had never
happened which almost made it not worth it,

water crashing against
the rocks the dull cry

almost, and so he played it in his mind like
a slow motion replay over and over as he got

of shovel blade into
soft earth the thud

of earth and scrape of
shove and the scream

of the man still playing
in their ears like on

a scratched record
a hundred years later

older until the thing had been played so often
that it had lost its sound and he forgot the

screams and the way the water had flashed
past the rocks and the dull scrape of the shovel

and the heavy groan of the body and all he
remembered was the sky, coolly distant, and

the way empty gray light had fallen
like dimes around his shoulders.

went fishin with howie and dean together one time

                                                                  never did that no more

    howie couldn't do nothin right

                                          couldn't tie a line, knocked our tackle box into
the water

          dean kept barkin at him to siddown

                                   later i heard from myrtle that,
after they got home, howie run into their backyard n wrapped his arms
around th honey locust tree, pullin on it, as if to rip it from the ground, or like to
try n get it to hug him back

                         turned into a great wrestler, though, big n strong
used to dive at th legs a th other boys n topple em like he was chainsawin
trees, n would always look over at his father after every pin like he was
waiting for some look that would say he was as good as miles, but that look
never come—dean would just stare back, his face blank as n elderly douglas fir

          weren't enough wrestling wins in the world to earn his father's approval
one afternoon match, howie twisted a quileute boy's arm so far around that
wqgtyou could hear th snap like a dry branch all through th cold gymnasium

                                                th kid
started screaming, kickin like a hooked salmon

                                   dean smiled, as though proud a
what howie done, but howie, face pale, knelt next to th boy, n cried th whole
way home

                 next day, he drove himself down to the rez to apologize for what he
done, n that's how come he met uma black, n they started seein each other,
datin, which is the worst thing ever happened to her

                                     uma had long dark
hair n half her face was purple from a burn she'd suffered on a hot stove n a
black spot on one eye n like howie had great wide shoulders like a football
lineman

                 she threw a mean fastball, too, n would pitch to howie on the
reservation ball field, would roll the sleeves of her sweatshirt up to her strong
elbows n shout swing, white boy! n overhand soggy baseballs across th paper
plate they used for home plate

                                after, he'd lie on his back on th wet grass, sunset
th color of th bottom of n aluminum pan, her head on the muddy whiteness a
th paper plate, n they'd feel th earth underneath them like ocean

                                        i'm a piece a
driftwood, he said once, gripping her hair in hi   s fingers like motorcycle
handlebars (n she felt her scalp tighten n imagined her skin coming off like a
sweatshirt, imagined herself a bonewhite skeleton lying on th baseball field)

II.

Here we are now,
entertain us.

—Kurt Cobain

In the Forest

gray light like ocean waves breaking in through the window   she sits in the
big soft orange chair, the pumpkin, they used to call it   the light off toomuch
gray light pouring in through the window   she remembers the rocky shore,
the rain, the winter waves, the pound and suck of the gray whitefoaming
ocean on the slick rocks   she remembers the raincoats in all the colors of the
flowers   marigold, rose, violet, green clover raincoats the bobbing heads of
her rainsoaked family—her father, her mother, her older brothers miles and
howie, her, then little brad—marching up and down the beach in the rain,
shepherded by their father, climbing on waterlogged driftwood, sliding off
rainsoaked spraysoaked driftwood, wet bark coming off in their cold pink
hands or feelingless mittens, the sudden water and foam curling around her
boots   in dreams she remembers being pulled out to sea, out to the ocean
with the whales and the cruel curving salmon and the fishing nets and the
blank gray coastguard boats and the buoys the color of orange sherbert-and-
vanilla ice cream and then the ocean beyond that—nothing but great endless
ocean until japan, until guam or okinawa and she remembers being swept out
and almost drowning in the peaceful gray light whalethick underwater
although her mother swears to her it never happened. Then how do I
remember it? she asks, sitting in the soft orange chair, the pumpkin, in her
mother's living room her mother has turned on the lamplight, pushing the
toomuch gray light out the window   walls solidifying squarely around her

Cold studio. A different light, whitegray, leaking through the old windows. She
studies her painting. Cedars, a rotting fence, a bear in the forest, the hint of a
house because of chimney smoke. Her bear looking more like a dog, her cedars
looking like droopy hippies; only the fence looking good, looking right: a rotting,
mossy fence that runs the perimeter—her father's words, there—of the house,
separating the inner yard from the outer yard much like the Lord dividing the
firmaments of the waters—her father's words, there. I have got to stop
thinking like that, she says, out loud, into the cold room, into the gray light
seeping through in the early afternoon, into the ear of the painting, that is to
say, into nobody and nothing, except for her, that is to say, into everybody she
knows and the grayish walls of the cold room. The fence is right, and
everything else is cloudy, confused—I can't even get a cedar tree right, she
says, looking at their slumping bodies. Peace, man, she says, holding up two
fingers, resisting the urge to tear it up, to tear it all into shreds, resisting the
urge to start over—yet again—with the peacefulness, the purity, of the white
canvas, the emptiness, the sense of possibility, moving to a new town—yet

21

again—like the beginning of a new painting, nothing like the beginning a new painting, she thinks, remembering her thesis advisor telling her, you have to stop always beginning, and she resists the urge to tear and shred and start over, she steps away from the canvas; she folds her arms across her chest, feeling again with awareness the lightness of the brush in her hands, how unlike an axe, how unlike her father's axe, and she remembers that grin, which even as her father grew older, as his hair went from black to gray to white, as his body went from solid to fragile to leukemia to papery lightness and then gone, like he was becoming like the light itself, the white light of an overcast day, like he'd never died, like he'd simply become sky and emptiness and disappeared, dissolving into Jesus, or nirvana, either/both. No. That wasn't true. She'd been at his funeral, but she never remembers it like that: although she remembers the piles of brown earth, the finality of soil, what she really remembers when she thinks about him is the vacation house on the straits: the blue sky, and the beach grass. The small white house overlooking Canada, and the strawberry beds, and the windsock, and the glass buoys lying in rocks around the house, and the daisies and the sturdy mailbox and the solid white unmossy fence. The rusted wagon wheel next to the latched gate and the endless fields of yellow flowers flowing away from the house. Her father utting white radishes with his pocketknife, whistling a hymn, and there'd be a plane in the sky, maybe, and starlings and sea gulls and crows harassing a bald eagle. I should paint that, she thinks, but she won't. She knows she won't. She could never paint something so beautiful, so clean and pure and blue and airy and pleasant and unforested and unchimneyed and unsmoky. Don't think that way, she tells herself. You've had three shows, she reminds herself, and although two were in a friend's restaurant, two of her paintings had sold for seven hundred dollars, total, and she liked to think of where they might be, now—in a living room, or probably not, her work was not really living-room material, probably a back bathroom, or work space, really, maybe a hallway piece. Stop thinking that way, she tells herself. She remembers sitting in her parents' living room and saying, Then why do I remember it? The water, the taste of seawater. I remember being pulled out by this big, powerful current. Like arms dragging me away. I remember how you and Dad looked, and Brad was there, too, holding his red plastic shovel. I don't know, sweetie, her mother says. I've heard about false memories, like too much psychology sessions cause patients to remember things that never happened. Psychiatry, she tells her mother, not psychology. And I really don't think I'm making this up. Her mother laughs into her cross-stitching. I would have remembered if my only daughter was being swept out to sea! Her high, clear, beautiful laugh like her beautiful singing voice—so opposite of her strong body—singing and playing the piano, leading the church choir. She says, Sweetie, are you sure it wasn't something where you were playing in the surf and the waves just seemed big? *Maybe,* she replies. *Maybe. But she'd been out to sea. She'd been out to sea.* She remembers the gray drowning waves, the massive gray drowning waves, the feeling of the whales close by, the feeling of an orange octopus drifting past. The waves like giants, grainy silty sea-water-green-gray giants, the pull of the current, the feeling of God and not-God right there, massive and pulling, and motherly and fatherly and all- ocean and all-sky and there was no protectiveness, there was no human concern, there was only nature, and it was massive and gray and oceanic and it was all life and all death and it stretched all the way to Japan and encircled the earth and that was God, not the loving, forgiving Jesus; not the violent, homophobic Paul, not any of the testaments. God was nature, and it/she/he wasn't good and it/she/he wasn't evil it just was what it was, *I Am,* or whatever, she thinks, now, in the cold rented studio space. *I'm not Buddhist I'm not Christian I'm not anything I am what I am. Okay, Popeye,* she tells herself while looking at the painting. *I yam what I yam.* She laughs. *When someone asks what I am I'll tell them I'm Popeye,* she says out loud into the cold air, standing with her brush in her hand, airy, light, her arms folded.

Brian's soft brown eyes, and they'd shattered. She'd had them all to herself, and held his face all to herself; those eyes had looked at her, and she'd let them look at her, and she could write a book about them: how they were brown, but with a little green in the center, a little fleck of seagreen. They'd used to kiss for hours, open-eyed, and then pull back and look into one another's eyes for what also seemed like hours, candlelight and lilacs and the spring smell of lupine and through the open windows the smell of the sea. His soft beard nice on her face, his eyes everywhere, always holding her, all the time, his skinny arms surprisingly strong, his body that seemed to barely weigh one hundred pounds, and then he'd hold himself sideways on a telephone pole. Brian with the bracelets he was always weaving; his stories about broken-down trucks in Costa Rica or Thailand, Brian with his Carhartts and his vegan eating except every now and then he would buy a dozen eggs and eat them all in one sitting, grinning and smiling the whole time. He ate chocolate so dark it was like eating charred wood—at least to her—and she remembers again his eyes, and the way she'd broken them. *Shattered his eyes like clay pots. Her. She'd done that. She'd shattered him.* She's high from pot smoke, sitting in her room she's renting with the door closed, even though no one else is in the house—her snowbird roommates/landlords both in Mexico, opening a café. She sits in her room with the window open and inhales smoke from her glass pipe in the shape of a lizard and then exhales through the open window into the mist and the baldhip rosebushes and the lilacs starting to turn brown, which means it's been two full years since she'd shattered his eyes. He's somewhere along the Pacific coast, that's all she knows, because he can't be ever anywhere else, permanently, either. He'd felt about the Pacific the way she'd felt about the Pacific, and he felt about the forests, and the bears, and the ice, and the rain, and the waves, and the smell of cedar smoke, and the smell of baldhip roses and lilacs and lupins and the poppies the way she did, as well, and they'd both hated the invasive Scotch broom, and they'd both hated the soul-deadening electronics and freeways and chain stores and brand-name clothes and airplanes and high-rises and skyscrapers and quick marts and food deserts and cement cement cement everywhere in this fucked-up cement world, they'd agreed. Concrete is for gravestones, would be his final word on the matter, and she'd push in closer to him underneath their heavy quilts, candlelight flickering in the breeze, her on top of him, his surprisingly hairy chest, his bony hips, his shinbones and anklebones underneath hers like a river current and then his hands would find her breasts, her nipples, and she'd resist, hold back the water behind the wooden logjam as long as she could before letting it break and flood the riverplain. Oh god, she'd say, as he moved underneath her, inside of her, and as she came she always saw an image of the Elwha floodplain: a braided creek; rock; cottonwoods spiring into the blue sky—then the grayness nothingness emptiness everythingness of the ocean. She exhales pot smoke. She feels rivers in her veins. She feels the trees, moving in the wind. She feels sockeye salmon paddling in the water. She feels pain but the absence of pain at the same time. The pot smoke allows her to remember Brian's face sharply and clearly: and it allows her to remember everything about Brian, and it also dulls the pain enough that she can remember everything about Brian but be distanced from it so she can think about it. She can even see his face, perfectly, in her mind. It was your choice, she reminds herself. She can imagine everything about him—when high—except of the thought of him with someone else. She can't, even though it's been two years—surely he must have, by now. No one can wait two years. Fuck that Penelope stuff. Impossible. She certainly wasn't waiting. Course, she wasn't getting Elizabeth-type sex, of course. Slut, she thinks. And yet Brad is so proud of his youngest daughter, always talking about her. She should tell him. Should tell him what Elizabeth is really like. Forget the blond ringlets, the politeness, the smiling. Except she likes Elizabeth—everyone does. How can you not like her. At least Brad actually is the squeaky-clean Christian he claims to be. She loves Brad, too. Everyone does. The younger brother who feels like the solid older brother, like an oak. Her: more like…maybe a river otter, sunbathing. Then swimming. Unable to make up its mind. That's what you otter do, she tells herself, something she and Brian used to always say. They had so many sayings they'd made up, the meanings of which were known only to them. And she'd left him.

For what reason? She takes a deep hit, holds the smoke, lets it slowly out her mouth out the open window into the Port Townsend spring. She lies back on her bed. Looks at her shelf of books. Plants of the Pacific Northwest, 101 Northwest Hikes, Alaska and Me, The Goddess Is Alive, Remedy Herbs, Siddartha. Even a copy of the Bible, more as a conversation piece than anything. Let me tell you about my family…A handful of Nancy Drew mysteries. She sits up, crosslegged, remembering how Brian would sit the same way. He had no bones. Flexible as rope. When they did yoga—and she considered herself fairly flexible—she felt like a wooden post compared to him. Once, they bought a book of knots and tried to see how many he could twist himself into. He got into all of them except for one, the Bowen knot, which he justified by saying, It's not a real knot, which they both shortened, over time, to, It's not a knot! Which they used as shorthand to describe any situation in which what it seemed was not what it was, until she ruined it at the end, she thinks, by using it to describe their relationship, It's not a knot, she'd said, and it was that, finally, that had made it clear to him that it was over, and that's when his brown eyes had done the pottery-shattering thing, and she'd seen it and she could never unsee it because she'd caused it. The sudden, total breaking. A human feeling clay-pot-shattering pain because of her presence in his life. She looks out the window. Wind nudges the lilac bushes and the rhododendron bushes, and the whispering sound sounds good, pure, in the uptown silence of the spring night. It happens, she tells herself. Every relationship, she thinks, is its own island, with its own coastlines and trees and cabins and piers and tide schedules and each of those things is known only to the people in the relationship, and sometimes not even by them, she thinks. Father daughter, mother daughter, blue skies and and low white peaceful clouds and the orange windsock and the rusted wagon wheel and the white picket fence and the fields endlessly stretching away and sometimes they flew kites—owl-shaped, or gull-shaped, or simple triangle shapes that her father built in his shed out of paper and wood and glue but somehow they hung together against the wind. Brian. And his eyes. (She sits in the living room with her mother in Forks and watches the rain outside. I miss your father, her mother says. And she says, Really? You do?) She hasn't seen her mother since that afternoon. Really? You do? She steps back from the painting. The bear looks like a dog. Even the fence, she now sees, looks watery. But the chimney smoke: she's captured the smoke. She remembers smoke from a beach campfire when she was still with Brian, she remembers rainlight soaking her sleeping bag. She remembers sitting up up and looking out at the offshore seastacks. Wind whistles through a hole in the buoy. The sand is wide and wet and dissolves into fog. Brian's sleeping bag is empty—he's somewhere out there, hidden from her, invisible, ghostly, but there. She pees strong in a small clearing where they've agreed to pee. She restarts the fire. She doesn't want to walk, doesn't want to go off into the fog, she wants to stay here and read and drink tea and then Brian will come back and they'll make love in this beautiful gray silence.

Alaska. At a bar, she listens to a long-haired woman strum two chords, back to front, back to front, and sing, and she drinks whiskey and listens to the woman sing, her long hair hanging down, her guitar held in her arms like a baby and the whiskey is warm and good and she has another, and then a third, the lanterns flickering off the windows as if dancing for their reflections only, and rain spatters against the windows, and everyone in the bar sways together, like a forest in the same wind. She eats salmon and warm bread and meets other fishermen and switches to beer, and they talk about the oceanic highways that the salmon travel, and one of them tells a long wandering story about a bear, a story that she can't quite follow, because although she's switched to lemon water now she's drunk, and two of the men walk her home and she knows they're safe and they know she knows they're safe, and they help her to her cedarwalled room, and she grabs both of them around their flannel collars and the two men look at each other, and then shrug, and they crawl naked into bed with her, three bodies warm together, and she nests between them both, pulls them all around her. In the morning one of the men tells her—the other has left—that his name is Brian. He smiles at her the brown of his eyes and she slides closer to his bony frame, a bird sliding in its twiggy nest at the top of a fir. (She sits in her bedroom in the spring, studying the books on her shelf and thinking about Brian. She sits in her parents' living room. Really? You do? In her rented studio she studies her painting—the hippie-like trees, the watery fence. The only thing she's captured perfectly, she thinks, is the smoke.)

Beaver Valley Homestead—1966

(grass buckles in the wind)   (gravel settles behind wheels)

        (the cattle on a thousand hills are mine)

  (grain the color of nickel in dull sunlight)

        (worn overalls hang off the whitewashed porch railing)

(with a farmhand he brands sullen calves)

    (weathered fences stagger like drunks)

(grain silos)   (she rests thin ankles on the porch railing)

(she stares at the birch trees)

        (they hold her down on the weathered porch)

  (he brands his initials on her spindly legs)

                (sunflowers burst)

(he dreams of gunmetal fields of grain)

(sky the color of cow's milk)   (the cattle on a thousand hills are mine)

        (the spray of hard gravel)

      (burst of sunlight)

  (she fights against the thick whiskey-smelling forearms of the men)

                    mercy

(white sheets hung from clotheslines shiver in the wind)

  (grain the color of metal)

   (the smell of burning flesh is like the smell of rusted tractor)

(in dreams he tries to embrace her but it's like holding onto a wind-billowing sheet)

       (she dreams of the spindly fingers of birch trees clutching her hair)

 (weathered porch)   (he envies the cattle fenced-in by weathered railings)

(she awakens from dreams of roaring tractors   his leg a cold flagpole in the bed)

     (in worn overalls he watches her hang sheets and listens for the approaching truck)

(faded sunlight on fields of grain)

      (a man with shoulders set against the rusted tractor)

(the cattle on a thousand hills are mine)   (she dreams of clouds)

        (two men wipe rust-smelling sweat from foreheads)

mercy   (birch trees)

    (sunlight gray on the weathered fences)

Robin

sparks from a campfire   robin a struck match in the honey locust tree she falls from
the nest   rain drums hard on the solid cedar roof   fourteen miles
toward town she pulls off the highway onto a forest service road robin flits
on branches   she fishtails up washboard gravel through the fog to a rock
cairn hidden in the nettles   she changes out of presbyterian-gray underwear
nto the silk and flash of red panties

the peppery smells of cedar   robin the color of riverside alders   robin abloom
in the forest   a crowded party   the smells of rust and smoke   she leaves
with a coastguardsman   they drive through the forest at daybreak
    robinsong like a stream over rocks   they hear the tapping sounds of a pileated
woodpecker in the aisles of the grocery store   they drive to a morning coast the
color of cantaloupe

the buzzing of gnats   robin wipes fog off the bathroom mirror   sunday
morning   perched on the stiff branches of aging cedar pews, robin mouths
the words of the hymns   robin stands in hip waders, madrona trees above her
rust-red on the hillside   she feels the coastguardsman coming inside her the
way seafoam rushes up the rocky beach   robin flutters off a stump and
tears a worm from the soil

the flare of robins in the trees   she drives south   warm seafoam on a sandy
nbeach   mojitos   cabanas   abdomen swollen   pregnant, she lays eggs and
curves to the earth for worms   returning to the northwest, robin stands behind
the counter at a liquor store, underage kids smile brightly in thick jackets and
low-hanging jeans   robin chirps and relents and sells them foamy beer
—rainier, olympia, budweiser, red stripe

robin's flight a rainbow blue eggs crack   daughters hatch   robin stands
hand in hand with her daughters on a windy beach   they unspool kites into
the wind until the skies darken   droplets of rain run down her oily
windshield   robin dark hair orange shirt gray jacket   robin gorges on
firethorn berries and walks drunk and dancing at night through the forest of
her blissfully manless house

robin's daughters dart downward from the nest   she drops them off at a
junior-high party   she pulls bangs the color of paper bags out of their eyes
robin's daughters wave her off   robins like red flares bloom in the forest like

madronas   passing alone uptown through sitka spruce a red-tailed hawk
screams and robin guns the gas pedal and flies through snags and pawn shops
until she's lost him, her heart pounding

daybreak   fishermen barbecue oysters outside wooden shacks   elk wash their
cars in driveways   the forest spills down to the rocky beach   mist blows in
off the ocean   and it's all robin can do to steady herself against the beauty
and terror of being a human, or a robin, in this forest, in this time   and robin
descends on a bonewhite madrona snag, and robin turns up the radio in her
car, and robin sings

n he'd keep reaching into his letterman's jacket to finger the draft card worn
smooth by his fingers, wishin it would just crumble like n alder leaf
    uma was a terrific football player herself

                                        played against her cousins
    they hit each other hard, bodies solid as cedars n when they found out about
howie they hit her harder, to teach her a lesson—but it didn't do no good cause
she hit back harder

                        laid inta james soeneke so hard she broke his collarbone, n
they had to carry him gently offa th field

                                    she'd go to baseball games n watch
watch howie charge around third n slam into th catcher

                                                n discovered she
enjoyed the sight a white people hurting one another, n was glad that howie
was leaving, so she wouldn't have to break up with him, n at the same time
hoped he stayed safe

                    after spring games his senior year she n howie'd still lie
on the infield, surrounded by nootka roses glistening wet, but it wasn't the
same as before, so they'd go for a drive in howie's parents' plymouth n go down
to the coast n sit in the front seat n stare across the strait to canada, n she'd say,
take a canoe and just paddle, all night, and when it's morning, you'll be there, n
howie

            then howie graduated n then he was gone

                                    it was nineteen sixty-eight
    myrtle dealt with his absence by cleaning

                                she rose early to survey the house
and, no matter how spotless it looked, at least to her youngest son ben, she'd tug
chemical sprays from underneath th sink n roll th sleeves a her flower-print
shirts up to her strong elbows (on weekends, if the youngest lingered too long in
the kitchen, she'd drop a bottle of bleach inta his hands n shoo him inta th
driveway to kill moss

                        there, he'd pretend he were a chinook helicopter, flying
low over viet cong positions, dropping napalm onto enemy villages, re-enacting
battle scenes that he read about in his brother's letters or saw on the evening
news, where he sat cross-legged—they still called it indian-style, at th time
—in front of dean's easy chair, watchin th early-evening westerns—pistols firing
into pine forests, stealthy indians, blank-faced cowboys riding on horseback—
become, seamlessly, footage a th war: m-sixteens firing into dense jungle cover,
stealthy viet cong, the frantic thrum of blank-faced helicopters)

                                                n uma went
for long early-morning walks, would watch th outlines of alders step forward
like bodies, hear th metallic calls a birds, sit on a wet stump, light a cigarette, inhale
smoke, n think about soeneke

31

III.

Una nueva racha de lluvia
se descarga contra los vidrios

> —*María Luisa Bombal, "La última neblina".*

Firs

the coast shudders from the weight of the tide   firs sculpted by the raw coastal
wind   he walks the long sidewalk   clovers grow thick   he plunges his hands
into more four-leaf clovers than he's ever seen   emerges with jeans grass-
stained at the knees, at the elbows of his jean-jacket   four-leaf clovers clutched
in his hand like a bouquet   he pulls at his short military haircut with his free
hand   as if to speed it along   he descends down the downcurving road   the
whitefoaming tide heavy on the rocky winter shore   the town   the fishing
boats   the rattling telephone wires and the fir branches bent landward
against a lifetime of wind   and then she's opening the door   and he's offering
her the bouquet of clovers   and she's laughing and shutting the door behind
him and she's closing out the gray light   they sit in her wallpapered kitchen
and drink burnt whiskey and they drink what's left of a plastic bottle of scotch
and watch the seahawks lose to the houston oilers seventeen to three   he feels
the weight of her meaty thigh solid against his own   his tired legs thin as fir
trees standing alone in a high wind

she sponges dark blood out of the baby's mouth   she rocks the baby on her
knee   he sits at the kitchen card table   headache resting on his hands   his
long hair spills to the floor   their two older children jump on sofas   toys
    carpet   a fuzzy football game playing on the television   he hears crashing
plastic trucks   she holds the receiver of their new phone in the crook of her
shoulder, talking to her mother   the baby, colicky, has been spitting up
something the color of motor oil   the baby tries to throw himself out of her
arms, then slumps heavily against his mother's shoulder like a bag of wet sand
        at the kitchen table he stares across dirty tupperware dinner dishes at the
wallpapered wall   irises   violets   toaster   calendar   refrigerator   magnets
    polaroid pictures   assembly of god stickers   dried clover scotch-taped above the
kitty wall-clock with the eyes that move   smooth counter   canisters of sugar
    canisters of flour   she sits down in the chair kittycorner from him and she
rocks the now-quiet baby   he threw it all up, she says, smiling   he rubs his
eyes, feels something go light within him   he reaches for the baby   you didn't
happen to see the score, didya? he asks   fourteen to six, eagles on top, she
whispers, and together they exhale, the way a sudden wind rushes through the
bodies of coastal firs

A Deer in the Salal

the ocean at high tide, she runs on the trail   salal walls thick on either side of
her   the wind overhead tearing branches from the firs   at the café, she serves
an elderly man coffee   he coughs and spits on the newspaper spread out on
the table   she shoulders through salal into a small clearing   raging wind
through the firs   the salal still and calm all around her, her daughter
following her through the thicket and nuzzling against her   she drives on a
wet highway, headlights ahead of her on the road, her daughter strapped into
the carseat in the back, neither of them knowing where they're going, all their
clothes and their lone dresser also in the back   the heat on low   the warm car
    the cold wind   again, he taps the porcelain coffee mug with a nickel   she
refills his cup   steam rises   his head bowed low against the newspaper like a
broken fir branch hanging raw in the wind   she steps into the thicket of the
kitchen   the protective door swings shut behind her to wall her safely inside
    they're short-handed today, just her waiting tables this morning   she takes
two plates of buttery pancakes   the cook glances at her   wind kickin up out
there, he says   she nods and backs out through the door   she runs on the trail,
    salal walls on either side of her   waves pound the rocks   oceanspray   the
rip of wind through the trees   she curls around her daughter in the salal   she
drives on the blank highway, her daughter curled in the back   she sets the
pancakes in front of the young couple in carhartts   they inquire about the
syrups   blueberry, raspberry, maple, she recites, but the four-top by the
window with the child in the booster seat is waving to get her attention   the
shed boy tucked in the back is ready to order   the table from the six-top is still
piled high with dishes like foaming waves   an island couple, their camper
parked outside like a whale, waves their check like branches in the high wind
    the elderly man taps on his mug, louder, hey you, he calls, also tapping his
cane   be there in a minute, hon', she calls back, yes, she says, to the young
couple in the carhartts, we have boysenberry   she runs on the trail   the wind
bites the branches of the firs, pounds through the solid arms of the madronas
    the wind rips trails through the rough beds of the kinnikinnick   there is no
sound but wind and the slash of oceanspray in sunlight   on her way to the
four-top and the island couple she has to pass the elderly man   this coffee's
cold, he says, as she goes by   she looks at the steam rising   i'll bring another
cup, she says, still moving past him   he grabs her arm   coffee station's that
way, sweetie, he says, his blue eyes rheumy, the crossword scribbled with
words in blue ink without regard to the placement of the white boxes   his grip
tight as a fir branch on her arm, she thinks about her daughter, thinks about
the empty table he's going to leave her instead of a tip   she feels his cold hand
and thinks of her father, the way his hands were similarly cold, near the end,

36

the way his eyes couldn't focus   the wind beats against the windows of the café   she runs on the trail   she drives on the wet highway, headlights ahead of her on the road   the heat on low   the warm car   her daughter strapped nto the back   neither of them knowing where they're going, but going together, nestled together in a thicket against the wind

Rain: A Sonnet

1.

no codes   no permits   four walls   a sloping mossy roof gutters swollen with
wet fir needles   davy raping nicole in the bedroom and i can hear her screams
over the rain falling onto the roof into the gutters and speaking in tongues on
the rosebushes and the plaid couch's rusted springs   boxed television   blue
walls   i can hear nicole's now-muffled strugglings but i've been smoking the
peppery spices of methamphetamines for three days and four nights, and all i
can do is stare out at the firs, gently swaying, in the invisible wind   davy
the boat mechanic   davy with the pickup truck   davy with the chainsaw
and the aluminum boat   we sit in the boat and toss nets or crab pots into
the oil-colored water   we lie on the soggy beach   we eat clam with butter and
meaty red wine   davy and i we pull trout out of rivers   davy and i we clear
brush and trim hedges and there's talk of a raise for me and davy's raping
nicole so i cover my ears with the soiled pillow   rain drips from gutters   the
wind bats sea gulls like baseballs   waves shudder hard against the continental
shelf and moss clings to diseased alders on the other side of the empty road
    like it's afraid to let go   like it's afraid it's going to fall a long, long, way

2.

on one day, at one town along the long unending wet coast we work the length
of a stone-blue day for this widow   she grows tomatoes fat as baseballs and
fall into my bucket   at night we hold her down on the bed, her face
muffled by a dacron pillow, pictures of her deceased husband and four
grandchildren watching in churchy silence from the bedside table   i spend all
day in the garden picking tomatoes and repairing the mossy fence
    davy gets up on the roof with a bucket and hose and cleans the gutters of fir
needles   the widow's bathroom is nice: pink rug, wicker shelves for magazines
and condensed books   at one point during the day i stand on the soggy earth
and shout up at davy, davy, i go, do you believe in god?   he stares down at
me for a long time, stroking the black stubble of his beard with the back of his
glove   i don't know, he says, do you?   i shrug and we stand looking at each
other for awhile before we go back to work   the sky is blue but darkening
wind hard off the coast   the widow's headlights scrape the driveway   a
rusted weathervane in the shape of a rooster stares silently at me   the house
the color of blue   the sky darkens   i tug tomatoes from vines and carefully
places them into the pail

3.

one time, during a heavy storm, davy screws an otter   we're loading a bagful
of em into the back of davy's truck in the rain, and he drops his rainpants, then
his darkblue sweats, and helps himself into the otter   you gotta do this, he
moans, as he thrusts   it feels unbelievable   better than a woman, in fact, he
says   he'd said the same thing about deer, though, which had turned out not
to be true and so i go around to the passenger seat and sit in the cold cabin and
shut the door and wait for him to finish   when he gets in, he goes, you missed
out, man   please tell me, i say, that we're not gonna sell that one   oh, we
are, he says, grinning his toothless grin, all black gaps and beard   we're gon
charge extra, he says   there was no wind, that day   just rain and then
the end of rain and long wet highways bluing in the weak winter light and
trees that knit their fingers together above us as we drove   we were in ocean
shores, then, both for that and for the widow, and for the story i'm about to
narrate   we were in ocean shores, on the long broken coast of washington
state

4.

we'd landed jobs in ocean shores with a landscaping company and in those
times, on gray sunday mornings, while davy would sleep, well, i'd like to go
down to church   there's something about the hard polished wood of the pews
worn smooth, something about the piano and the hymns and the grape juice
and the saltine crackers, something about the air inside the buildings, that
calms me   all things bright and beautiful, we sing   all creatures great and
small   all things wise and wonderful, the lord god made them all!   and it's
true   all things bright and beautiful, that's me and davy, our veins full   we
sit in his boat, the sunlight beautiful on the oil-colored water, and we pull the
whiteness of of crabs out of the darkness into our boat, and we pull out chum
salmon with fishing line, and we hit them on the head, once, to still them before
tossing them into the briny buckets   we weedeat blackberry and vine maple
     we pick and prune on the beautiful earth   we smoke and wrap our arms
carefully with air hoses and then—how to describe it? the earth begins to shine
     and my teeth stop hurting and i'm rushing downmountain strapped to the
rusted hood of davy's truck and the truck has no brakes, like falling through
empty sky toward empty sky   and the birds are all bright in the trees and
beautiful and wise and wonderful and all the creatures make sense to me as i
fall and in those moments i even forget jail

5.

after church one sunday there's a potluck, which this church has on the first
sunday of every month   there's buttered corn on the cob, beans,
homemade coleslaw on soggy white paper plates   there's red, white, and blue
bunting hanging off the white picket fence that surrounds the side of the
church facing the ocean   we sit on the thin picnic table benches and eat   and
it's good   there's white cake and watermelon slices and jellied peaches for
dessert and a large whale-sized woman sits down across from me   the picnic
table lifts up gently as she sits, although my feet stay on the ground   she had
arrived late, she says, because of her kid, nicole   she eats cake and meat and
beans and wips her hairy chin   so, what's your story? she asks me   you
seem like you've had a hard life, bein all bone-rail thin   is that true?
    fisherman, i say   like jesus, she says   there's a pause   do you believe in the
lord? she dutifully asks me   i don't know, i say   but i'd like to   me too, she
says   my name is candy, she says   her arms are massive and short and her
bracelets glitter bright and beautiful in the sun

6.

we meet for coffee at mcdonalds   out the window kites scrape the air and cars
drive down the lonely pavement toward the hard-packed beach   it's ten o'clock
and they won't serve her hamburgers or fries until ten-thirty   but there's no
one else here, she says   that's not true, the cashier says, a goth-looking girl
with a tragic white face and piercings   she points out four older men sitting in
flannel and slacks, drinking coffee and talking politics in the corner   why
can't you go ahead and fire up the grill? candy asks   candy puts both hands
on the counter and her rings leave marks deep and ragged in the formica and i
think she's gonna start yelling but she doesn't   it was enough to destroy their
counter   she smiles and says, fine, and she orders cookies for while we wait
until ten-thirty   eat, she tells me   you need to put some meat on your bones,
you look like you'd blow over in a high wind   she has to leave at noon to
get back to her kid, so after I watch her drive away i walk north along the long
beach back toward the old motel   the dunes are salted with grass and cars
pass by me on the beach   i sit for awhile on a tire stuck in the sand and look
out at the frothy empty gray waves coming endlessly in   like we're all waiting
for something, but have no idea what we're all waiting for

7.

the kid we're buying from says he won't give any more until we pay   n we're
also overdue on our room   we're two hunnert n thirty short, davy says,
spreading wet bills and loose change on his bedspread   not counting what we
owe em for the last two months   i sit and smoke by the window, stub it out on
the wall   davy starts throwing his clothes into his duffel bag   i hear they're
hirin in aberdeen too, he says   some rich guy got lots of property to weedeat

40

gimme some time, i say   i'll get us some dough   i got some ideas, i say
and that's how come we end up standing huddled outside the church building,
the single whiteblue sodium light falling like the holy spirit himself around us
while candy fumbles with the key ring and we go inside   i keep my fingers
on her neck the whole time, cooing and massaging and telling her how much i
love her and she lets davy into the main office where he ransacks the place
candy and i wait in the sanctuary on the wooden pews   my finger up her
and she cries and i hold her and tell her i love her so much and on our way out
davy re-arms the alarm then locks the door and then kicks it in and we get in
his truck and drive away and the white alarm lights spread their wailing
hands around the inside of the sanctuary   candy sits in the middle of the truck
cab, arms around both of us, my hand on her thigh, not one of us in that
moment having any fun

8.

candy slices up salmon into flanks and grills it in lemon and paprika wrapped
up in aluminum foil   she sits and holds the tongs   davy and i we drink
whiskey and smoke and candy's thin teen nicole sits in the corner of the mossy
patio pretending to text or play games on her broken cell phone   later that
night candy and i are like two sea creatures under the bedspread and i hear
bedboards break and everything is salt and ocean and forest and wet and
warm rain and for some reason i think of the story of the thunderbird and the
whale, where thunderbird tries to get the whale from the depths of the ocean in
order to drop her from a great height crashing down into the woods   after
candy falls into an injected sleep i take the television apart and looking down
at the television, as i pull it limb from limb, is like looking down from a great
height like looking down at the mountains   and i hear davy and i hear nicole
struggling in the other room but it's so beautiful: the forest   the rain
thunderbird   the beautiful whale and ocean shores

9.

candy won't return my calls so i wait outside her house on her porch in my
down jacket   i wait   the rain falls down and each raindrop says my name
in a different way   i wait, and i wonder which is more: the number of words
spoken by all humans since the beginning, or the individual rain on the shore,
on the wet rocks, on the forests, on the beach grass   i think that it has rained
more than people have spoken   candy finally opens the door and her eyes
are red and tearstained   we sit across from each other at her kitchen table
and i tell her i love you   three words drowned out by the weight of all that
rain   candy puts her face in her hands and cries and i pouch my hands in
my jacket   her kitchen is cold and bible verses adorn the walls but now it's

like they're accusing me   i wish the words were rain   the walls are blue like
a yearning for the sky   i knew it, she's moaning   i knew it   each three-
word phrase erasing my own three-word phrase even more than the rain

10.

i blame davy   she's gone   they're both gone   drifting in the boat with davy i
steady the aluminum rails as he leans deep over the dark water to pull in the
crab pots   it would be so easy   davy drowning   davy spitting up water
the boat would be mine   candy would be mine   her sacrifice not in vain
so easy to put up my booted foot and tip him in   to take the motor   to
motor away under the gray lidded sky on the dark gray water   the yellow
sunset light rimmed at the edges only   kiteboarders lifting themselves into
the air and then back down again beyond the breakers outside the harbor
hard misty rain coming down like snarled fishing line   i hold the sides of the
boat   i sit in candy's kitchen and hold her hand as she cries into a dirty
dishtowel   i hold candy from behind in her kitchen while she stands at the
sink and stares out at the rain and she smells of baking powder and talcum
powder and i tell her, you can hit me, if you want   rain streaks down the
windows of davy's truck in rivulets   i sit in the harbor with davy surrounded
by shore on all sides, except for a thin path to the ocean

11.

candy asks me what I'm most afraid of   this is earlier that summer: we're in
snohomish   at the fair   we'd decided to drive up for the day, mostly just to
have time alone in her car   her daughter is walking around somehwere
with twenty-dollar bills we've each given her   we're rising up to the top of
the ferris wheel and we can see the addictive lights of everett and even seattle
the glow of city lights and the cobalt blue of the non-clouded summer sky and
my hand is digging around in her crotch   her in a stained white tank top, me
in a flannel shirt with the sleeves cut off, her head on my shoulder, i tell her:
abandonment, mostly   yeah, bein alone   she massages my thin chest and
belly through my shirt   we're down at ground level again and rising up when
she blows in my ear   you don't have to be alone, she says, you don't   i'm here
her wet mouth in my ear, so much pleasure that it's pain

12.

ocean water, endless   like god   ocean water, full of storms, of whales, of
cargo and navy ships   words mean nothing in the great context of the
ocean   actions mean nothing   right?   rain and ocean water is all there is
and nothing we do or say will be remembered because of the ocean and the

rain davy is leaning over and looking at the dark water   the rain has picked up and pockmarks the surface of the water as davy and i we pull crab pots into the belly of the aluminum boat   i think about candy and remember holding her and i look at davy and i want to push him in but i don't i just stare out at the gray whale-sized clouds, steadying myself in the boat because of the rocking motion

13.

in church we sang: all things bright and beautiful, and creatures great and small, all things wise and wonderful, the lord god made them all!   i felt candy's hand enveloping mine   i sat in wonder at the greatness of the ocean and the massive forests and the beaches and the groaning of the whales and the drowning quality of the rain

14.

no rain   warm evening   on the ferris wheel, we rise   we lift up out of the mells of cotton candy and cigarette smoke   we lift up out of the calliope noise   we lift to that feeling right at the top   right before you start to descend   that brief moment of floating where nothing else exists   nothing   no words   not even my name

n then soeneke he come back n uma opened her trailer door to his fragility n she let
him in

       howie come back, too (the red bruises of abandoned boxcars
blooming in the woods he walks along rusted railroad tracks, hands jammed in
his back pockets)

         but somethin was different (he leans against a wet chain-link
fence, drunk, and studies an empty can of busch beer lying in the weeds on the
outskirts of the parking lot but doesn't pick it up because then he'll have to pick
up the parking lot, as well, and then all the cars, and the five-and-dime, and the
gas station, and the propane gas tank, and the square houses huddled tight
against the rain, and the oceanic pull of wind in the cedars, and the aluminum
boats of the fishermen on the lake and the miles of wet sand, and the sea gulls,
and the rattling telephone wires, and the mossy alders, and the eagle's nests,
and the rocky offshore seastacks, and the gray raging ocean, and if he picks up
all those things there won't be anything left for him to stand on)

            at th bar he
complained loudly to about th faithlessness a women

          went to church with his
parents but spent th last service fore he died in a motorcycle crash starin at th
window at a wasp tryin to wrestle free from a cobweb

            (rain lashing his face he
screams around a wet corner, skids, th arrows a sodden alders entering his
leather jacket at a hunnert miles n hour)

        howie dated ruthie dawson's skinny
daughter frances pretty heaviy but the word was that he was rough with her
and called her uma when they did it

        (th night frances leaves him, th moon a
full white carving in th sky, howie throws a sodden case of budweiser into the
front seat next to him n pours it down his throat n swallows a greenie n drives
down to th coast, throwin empty beer cans out th window as he goes, drives
past th heavy bodies a douglas firs n cedars n spruces to th sodden edge of th
continent to th rez, churned gray saltwater and alder pouring into the truck
cab with him

     he stops in front a uma's trailer

        uma sees him through th window
n comes out trembling on painkillers, james n children asleep on th couch
 n they take a walk on the beach, a killdeer faking a broken wing to protect th
nest
   falls through the orange glow a old streetlights

          i'm glad you made it, she
says, truthfully

i missed you, he says, n he takes off his jacket n tries to wrap it around her, but she steps back, so he's just holdin it in his hands, n because he has nothin to say, he picks up a baseball-bat-sized stick pushed in by the surf n swings like he were about to dig in at th plate,

or maybe he'd brought the stick with him from th edge of th parking lot (he holds the stick like a bayonet, like a frontier rifle, like n m-sixteen), or maybe his father had given it to him over the years

IV.

All I can say
is that my life is pretty plain
I like watching the puddles
gather rain.

—*Brad Smith, "No Rain"*

Loon

head the dark color of a river eddy   body the ruffled white of wind-blown ice
sky slate gray and smoky like motorcycle exhaust   loon slams the faded door
of the water-colored house   loon sits on the motorcycle in the front yard   loon
revs the engine   clouds boil above the lake   loon swims webbed feet
thrashing the water beneath the surface   loon sits on his motorcycle   the
lake is freezing solid and he doesn't have enough water, his wings too slim to lift
without a long takeoff   loon remembers the crunch of pills   loon remembers
swallowing greenies   loon remembers the feeling as if being swept down a
hill   the sun shining on the snow   earth shining   loon remembers lifting
trucks over his head   a sudden god   the chalky taste of the pills   loon
remembers being able to lift off into cold gray air the color of mountains and
fly   loon paddles uselessly   cottonwoods glazed with ice   lake whitening
all around his slight body   the ice seals around him   the sun glints off the
gray pavement of the road leading away from the water-colored house   loon
leans forward   ignores the pressed faces clouding the window-glass   the
open red mouths   the howls of each dirty face   loon remembers looking
down on shining white snow   loon remembers how he could once hear the
thoughts of each individual fish or cottonwood   loon remembers how, free, he
could once feel the clouds coming apart like wet newspaper   and loon longs to
take off   and the dirty faces in the window, they wait in silence, wondering
what he will do

Quiet Water

wide blue straits   blue sky   the wide gray skirts of home depot and starbucks
stoplights   trimmed hedges   shrubs   she lies on her belly on their bed   he
plays madden, shouting, periodically, at the screen clouds schoon across the
sky   fog motors over the empty straits   rain spits down periodically   he pulls
scentless rhododendrons from clay soil   he trims back salal   she sits among
potted plants   telephones   computer keyboards   evening shopping
afterglow a thin red band on the horizon   four tomatoes for three dollars
wide glass counters   rotisserie chicken   potato salad   weekends they sit on
wide sloping fields   white wine in plastic glasses   they drive home unsteadily
on a little vicodin, a little weed   they make love like deer used to four stories
beneath them in a long-gone thicket   the numbers in their bank account tick
gently upward, their lives like ocean mist continuously dissolving into sunlight
and rain

A Final Memory

*truck sliding off gravel road   rabbit face of moon   shining blank face of
mountain   dark firs   crumble of clay soil through the open windows   blood
shattering of glass   they sit in the aluminum boat, nylon lines connecting them
to the water   worn seats soaked with rain   prow gliding through lily pads
he splashes after tiny green frogs   cupped hands   callused hands grip the
useless steering wheel of the truck   scent of lake water   they sit in the
aluminum boat shoulders hunched against the rain   white–and–red coleman
cooler   they slice trout open like envelopes, scrape pink intestines and scales
the color of hemlock bark over the side   the truck slides off loose gravel
them gone   one last warm memory of frogs and lake and trout then gone
and only the blank face of the mountain, and the rabbit face of the moon,
remain*

they cross th small stream that cuts from the salal down through the beach to
th blackness a th ocean

                      mist rifles through the tops a th wind-shredded firs
n he bends down n he tries to kiss her, but she pulls away, says, let's start
walking back

              fuckin faithless gook, he says, n as she walks away she tips her
face up toward the sky, as if to gulp th rain

                    he catches up to her, cradles his stick
on his shoulder, n smacks her face with it

                uma cups her mouth with her hands
  blood drips through her fingers, n she stares at him

                 all you gooks are so fuckin
stoic, aren't you, he says, well, i'll get a response

                    n only the driftwood and i hear
the snap of her cheekbone shattering, n of her teeth tossed across the wet sand
like dice

       no longer a man he's a bear

             he tackles her n tries to rip her jeans off,
holding her down, wide red mouth, a hairy paw around her throat, silver
worm of saliva, his belt around his knees, his grizzly nostrils exhaling steam
    —cept for, she's a bear too

                  n ain't no bear like a bear with cubs
  she claws him n tears his craggy face, n they roar on the rocky beach, two
bears raging on a wet foggy night on th northwest coast, lit by th weak orange
glow of streetlights from th town

         n he flees

                howie became completely a bear,
after that

      was no man left

            he'd roar at the bars, pull salmon outta their vehicles
n try n devour them, let his chainsaw roar in the forest

                but up until his death in
th alders there weren't enough salmon, weren't enough women, weren't
enough trees to chop in the entire forest to earn th love a this father

                      anyway,
enough about him

       i only saw uma once more, years later

               she was shopping at
the thriftway with two fierce young sons

             her hair was starting to gray, n i
wasn't even sure it was her

         it was like seeing someone you thought you knew,

but maybe you didn't

        like seeing someone you'd known once, but that person

was long, long gone

The trees, the rain, the people here are all true. We lived here for awhile and now some of us are gone, and those of us who are here will be gone someday.

Rain muffles our lives, here. Sometimes we're laughin but you can't hear us on account of the rain, n sometimes we're screamin but you can't hear us then, neither.

And the glaciers advance and recede, leaving no indication that any of us, any of us at all, were ever even here.

TEBOT BACH
A 501(c) (3) Literary Arts Education Non Profit

THE TEBOT BACH MISSION: advancing literacy, strengthening community, and transforming life experience with the power of poetry through readings, workshops, and publications.

THE TEBOT BACH PROGRAMS

1. A poetry reading and writing workshop series for venues such as homeless shelters, battered women's shelters, nursing homes, senior citizen daycare centers, Veterans organizations, hospitals, AIDS hospices, correctional facilities which serve under-represented populations. Participating poets include: John Balaban, Brendan Constantine, Megan Doherty, Richard Jones, Dorianne Laux, M.L. Leibler, Lawrence Lieberman, Carine Topal, Cecilia Woloch.

2. A poetry reading and writing workshop series for the Southern California community at large, and for schools K-University. The workshops feature local, national, and international teaching poets. Participating poets have include: David St. John, Charles Webb, the late Wanda Coleman, Amy Gerstler, Patricia Smith, Holly Prado, Dorothy Barresi, W.D. Ehrhart, Tom Lux, Rebecca Seiferle, Suzanne Lummis, Michael Datcher, B.H. Fairchild, Cecilia Woloch, Chris Abani, Laurel Ann Bogen, Sam Hamill, David Lehman, Christopher Buckley, & Mark Doty.

3. A publishing component to give local, national, and international poets a venue for publishing and distribution.

Tebot Bach
Box 7887
Huntington Beach, CA 92615-7887
714-968-0905
www.tebotbach.org